Otherwise Forgotten

Poems

Samantha Lord

This collection was previously published as *Pressed Flowers* by Samantha Lord in 2020.

Table of Contents

Pressed Flowers

I keep my poems
safe and pristine
concentrated

confined
like pressed flowers
in a book

and like one
of those dried and
fragile objects

they may crumble

Over My Shoulder

2

Over my shoulder
behind

my memories

a light shone
brightly
in the corner

of my eye —

the possibilities
of a moment

in my mind

I Am Not

I am but
I am not
in your view

I am not
visible outside
the lines
you have
an identity

for me
to occupy
I am not there

I am not

A Blank Wall [4]

What will
you do
when there
is simply
no poetry

inside —

when despite
all your
heroic efforts
the mindless
hum of

crowded life
has become
too much
and you
cannot hear
the whispers

within?

The Thinker

One who
has died
and is here
in disguise

one who
has died
but is the
only one

alive

The Open Window

The last time
the air had
this scent
I felt happy
as I walked with
the breeze

I opened
windows with
the freest
sense of possibility
and saw
renewal all
around me

The last time
the air had
this perfume
I could see
the past and
future meld into
the now
in a unity

I was powerful
I was wise

Isolation

I look to
the sky
whose tears
fall above me
whose soul
wants to love me
whose will wants
me to fly —

But I am human
and the window
closed

The Light Blinds

The light blinds
the window

obscures
the
world outside —

your
vision
is something less

than human, more
than mortal

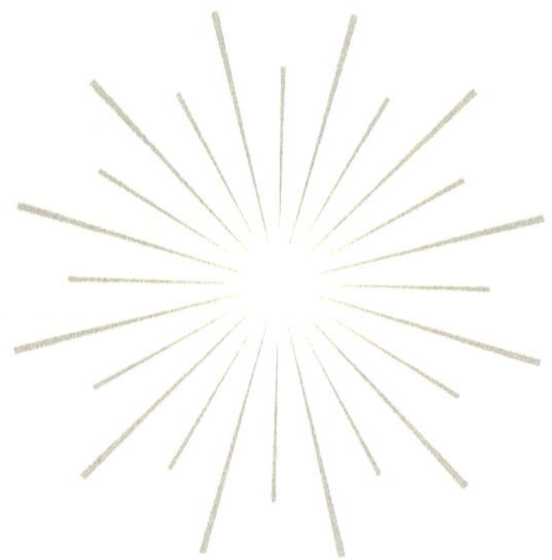

dazzling patches
of bright white
freeze time
motionless

widen
the gap
between heartbeats

A Matter of Patience

You said it
and so did they

it's just a matter
of patience
getting the things
   that sustain me.

it's just a matter
of time
   a hostile thing
   I can't control.

I'd say it
dissolves before
my eyes but
I've never seen it.

I look shyly
down from a
bright burst of hope
   high aloft
   yet again

The Coffee Sipped

The coffee
sipped she thought
of last night's dream

or nightmare
uncertain which
but it was true
it was real

now the sky
outside the window
is blue infused
with yellow

in her dream's time
it was inky velvet
almost solid —

stars peeked through
as if from behind
a velvet curtain

she sips the coffee
her new reality

11

Perhaps

Perhaps
the purpose
of poetry
is not

to describe
and illuminate
but to deeply
explore and
lightly imply

to hint
in a way
only experience
can understand

How Many

How many Emily Dickinsons
have lived and died
    their work thrown away
    with old furniture?

How many Vincent van Goghs
    unable to afford paint
    and a place to rest?

Different Legs

In this
same spot

I walked
with different legs
steadier breath

with simpler yet
limitless images
 ahead

I don't think I
noticed the rush
 against me

or if I did, I saw
it was all part
 of the plan

Bare Bones

Bare bones
and walls —
thin elliptic skin
couldn't stop can't
remember always

forgot

Always Forgotten

It's easy
to remember
but not to
feel the pink sky
fire amidst

the green overreaching
  light and lustrous

At Dusk

Misty, violet
revelation
rushing forward
spaces enclose
time withdraws
half huddle in

others venture out
soaring, exploring
under tree boughs

in shadows, the rest
can hide

Comfort

When thoughts
torment me
I must write
their foes —

I need a little
piece of paper
on which to
write a comfort

to fix in one
spot a truth
spinning in my soul

Falling Apart

It was startling
snaking up the façade
an invader
splitting shelter
in two

I saw you outside
staring at reality
watched you in profile
looking up
beside you

around you
you can hear
the fading of your
surroundings

a low unstoppable hum
replaced a heartbeat

Fragile

Poems
are fragile things

I pushed too much
on the fragments of one
leaving only
shimmer and dust

brittle and lifeless

Further

At once
we become
we move
further away
from and
closer to —

death
non-being
the blank canvas
from which we
emerge
the futile
or fruitful realm

dreams
possibilities
impossibilities
the spotless page
where we hope
to write
with a pen
entirely different

drifting and
falling — cloaked
with illusions
we move
forward

Heavy Sleep

The air
after a rainstorm
helps me
to breathe

anxiety is eased
and awe mellows
into enchantment

then
falling —

memories melt
me to peace
mingle with
the darkness

of thoughts
inspirit spaces
beneath sleep

casting
spells
deeply felt
and hazily seen
in dreams

White Noise

Falling asleep
cradled by a
solid hum
expanding
behind your eyes

noise that acts
as silence
setting you
in a steady line

then you begin
the seeing
and hearing
in your mind

Small Yellow Room

Sallow air pools —
the window view
a yellow like
gas light

was the room
on the second floor —
a fuzzy-like feeling
like fainting
or tasting the scent
of incense

in a mind palace
such as this

Silenced

My writing looks
uneven, uncertain
  shy

my brain seems
motionless
cannot seek
  doesn't find

my mouth is
free to open
but doesn't
it won't
  like in a dream

I struggle to speak
to scream, but
even if I could
what would be
  the point?

Shattered Wings

Feathers
brittle like
broken china

Span
the sparkling
wind — questioning air —
downward curve — hindrance

And
the bird
steadily falls, level
to level, slowly down
a
staircase

Poverty

In certain ways
I must be a realist

so that I may live
to be an idealist

My Reason

What's my reason?
I don't have one,
but you don't have me —

so here I am
with my useless book
in this quiet
studious room

The Last of Everything

The last of everything
and I'm lost
    to everything
    and anything
    you value

You don't see me
you see my eyes
    but not the thoughts
    that animate them

    you see my face but
    cast off the memories
    that are its creator
        with a casual sweep
        of your hand

Spotted Night

Luminous glides
through mottled spaces
lending clarity, stars

halo its slender frame —
    sparks hanging on the horizon

Revelation

As always
there's a flower
in the deep
dawn that enriches
my mind
with its mildness

I want this
    stillness, softness, coolness
to permeate my burning brain
    pulsating, beating
my soul fighting with itself

Gushing wind mixes
with a strong exhale
and dies near my fire

Gentle friend
shed me a soft tear

Walking

Against a cool
gentle breeze
amongst warming
sunrays

I walk alone
staring straight ahead
or watching my feet
as they move

Wearing the curious
self-contained smile
of a secret, floating

Last Light

Darkness creeping in
too quickly

walking home in
a different world

33

Déjà Vu

Messages from the past. Wisdom, perhaps from a dream. And the future as well. But I have an ambition for mysticism. I seek the cryptic. I want to see objects and events with spiritual X-ray eyes. Shapeshifting, fading in and out of the light, sinking back into the darkness.

There are seers outside, peering through the rain at our window. Like people of a magical ocean city looking up through the water's surface. They are weighed down by sadness yet live in exaltation.

The glowing eye, the serene expression, the quiet mind. They are part of our past as well as our present, our future, the realm of dreams. We have seen them so many times before.

Rejected Tears

Under
all — only me
searching for peace

enclosed by walls
whispering
in a storm of ice

I need to much for life —
I am wounded by a fire neglected
until quenched by sacrifice

35

The Window

Watching from a window, I saw leaves in the wind. Then walked on, crumbling to the earth. Later on, winter rain, incongruous and cruel. Yet beautiful. I reached out my hand — cold regeneration sinking into my skin. I thought of going outside by time passed. It passed so quickly.

I fell asleep on my bed beside the window and eternity filtered through my dreams. I saw essences rather than faces. The tree with roots that span the earth and branches that reach the sky. Long passageways with ghosts in the walls, pulling me in. Eventually I was awoken, warm breeze brushing my cheek.

Perhaps I will go outside. I watch this possibility through the window.

Heights

Through the
weighted curtains
ponderous glass
heavy air holding you in
contact is yet made
communion is there

A being sits on the rail
on the edges of
contained space

Its eyes amaze you
magical, it has reached
this height from the
humble ground

You shatter backwards
shaking from the dream

Compressed

Star-signals
building castles
on the surface
of my eye melodic

swirls flamed out
brought down to size –
advised to stay much
longer, a day, a week, a year

a life lost far within the circle
of what it could have been
timeless flight

The Water

There seems so much more of it,
its body rising up, pushing
against our walls,
enraged, alarming.

Every time I see the water,
it has gained on us,
as if it has absorbed

surrounding
suffering.

The greater damage done,
the more it will swell
until it overtakes
entirely.

39

Remember That

Remember that
bus stop you walked me
to on a static winter evening
all those years ago?
I'm still there.

The opaque denim sky
looming over

Bright Ghost

We do not see. You thought we could, thought we would release our eyes, open and absorb. You thought we might. We feel an energy behind us. The seeping quality of heat, the invasive nature of light. Like a fire, that offers both life and death.

There doesn't really seem anything to do, anywhere to go. But you know what, you know where. You turn to face the light, with courage unknown by most. Absorbed, you become our bright ghost.

This book was previously published
as *Pressed Flowers* by Samantha Lord
in 2020.

The following poems were also published in
chapbook, *Ghosts in the Walls* (2009):
"The Thinker"
"Isolation"
"Comfort"
"Heavy Sleep"
"White Noise"
"Poverty"
"Revelation"
"Walking"
"Déjà Vu"
"Rejected Tears"
"The Window"
"Mute"